WITHDRAWN
FROM STOCK

124347
£10.76

Chinese Fans

Artistry and Aesthetics

Gonglin Qian

LONG RIVER PRESS
San Francisco

Editorial Committee

Art Adviser: Yang Xin, Wang Qingzheng & Zhang Daoyi
Chief Editor: Wu Shiyu
Deputy Chief Editor: Ma Ronghua & Dai Dingjiu
Editorial Committe Members: Qian Gonglin, Lin Lanying, Zhang Debao &
Wushaohua

Author: Qian Gonglin
Executive Editor: Dai Dingjiu
Designer: Lu Quangen
Photographer: Ni Xiuling
Introduction: Dai Dingjiu
Translator: Huang Youyi
English Editor: Luo Tianyou

First Edition 2004

ISBN 1-59265-020-1

Library of Congress Cataloging-in-Publication Data

Qian, Gonglin.
[Shan zi. English]
Chinese fans : artistry and aesthetics / Gong Lin Qian.— 1st ed.
    p. cm. — (Arts of China ; #2)
ISBN 1-59265-020-1 (pbk.)
1. Fans—China—History. 2. Fans—Collectors and collecting. I.
Title. II. Series: Arts of China
NK4870.Q2513 2003
391.4'4—dc22

                        2003018304

Published in the United States of America by
Long River Press
3450 3rd St., #4B, San Francisco, CA 94124
www.longriverpress.com
in association with Shanghai People's Fine Arts Publishing House

Printed in China

10 9 8 7 6 5 4 3 2 1

Table of Contents

Introduction

*S*ince ancient times, the Chinese have used fans not only as tools to provide relief during hot weather but also as objects that embody the wisdom of Chinese culture and art. Fans have attained the highest form of excellence in handicraft art. They have also constituted a unique wonder of artistic style and have been gems of art in traditional Chinese culture. The exquisite paintings and calligraphy placed onto the fans, and the delicate and meticulous carvings on the fans, have made them highly valued collectors ' items. Stage performing artists use fans as props to add liveliness and subtlety to their performances: opening them, closing them, now holding them horizontally, now holding them vertically, etc. The shapes of the fans have even been used in architectural designs in the form of the open windows found in some of the world famous gardens of Suzhou. In fact, as a cultural form, the charm of fans has been demonstrated and utilized to the fullest extent. Though fans are common both in and outside China, Chinese fans boast a colorful history of development in the past as well as the present.

1. Fans and Their History

*R*ecords of fans fashioned from bamboo or even feathers are encountered in China's earliest recorded history. Tools and containers of woven bamboo were already used in primitive society in China. Neolithic era ruins dating from 5,000 years ago, which were unearthed from Qianshanyang in Zhejiang province, have yielded more than 200 pieces of woven bamboo utensils, ranging from baskets in various shapes, to mats employing complicated weaving techniques. The making of bamboo fans developed naturally and logically. What is especially enlightening is the fact that the lower level of the ruins at Qianshanyang have also yielded silk and hemp fabrics, including pieces of cloth, ribbon, and thread. Analysis reveals that these were produced from domesticated silkworms. The silk fabrics thus herald the emergence of silk fans and provide an important historical clue to the widely held belief that the legendary Chinese rulers may have had fans before the development of recorded history.

The earliest fans to have been found so far date to the Spring and Autumn and Warring States Period (c. 770-221 BC) and fall into two categories: those made of bamboo and those made of feathers. The short-handled bamboo fan unearthed from the No. 1 tomb of Mashan Brick Mill, Hubei Province, of the Warring States Period (475-221 BC) is the earliest actual evidence of a fan that has been found. According to the excavation report, written by the Jingzhou Museum, the bamboo fan was 16 inches long. The fan cover, or spread, was woven with very thin and refined black and red bamboo strips with rectangular patterns. There were two rectangular holes on one side of the handle. The borders of the holes were rendered with relatively thicker bamboo strips and with very neat patterns making the fan a highly artistic woven bamboo object.

An article prepared by the Cultural Relics Archaeology Institute of Hubei Province suggests that during the Spring and Autumn and Warring States Period, fans were made of either bamboo or feathers and were often used as burial objects in the State of Chu. Feather fans came in two types: the first were those with long, square wooden handles, pointed at one end and thick at the other. At the top horizontal and crescent-shaped bamboo strips created the basic form of a fan, whose cover was made by putting feathers together. The end of the feather's stem was tied by a silk ribbon to the wooden handle while the other end was tied to the bamboo chip. About two meters long, such a fan was too large to be held in an owner's hand and the job of fanning had to be left to servants. Such fans have only been found in several large and medium-sized tombs of the State of Chu, and they were obviously used only by the nobility. The other type of feather fans were short handled, with a pointed slanting top from where feathers formed the fan cover. These were fastened by a thin hemp or silk thread. The bottom was oblong in shape. Such fans were about 10-12 inches long and could be held in the hand for personal use. More than a dozen such fans have been found in small and medium-sized tombs of the State of Chu.

Two bamboo fans, one large and one small, were also found during the excavation of the No. 1 tomb at Mawangdui in Changsha, and have been dated to the Western Han Dynasty (206 BC-AD 23). The large fan was 70 inches in length while the small fan was 20.5 inches in length. The fan spread was terraced in shape and closely woven. The bamboo strips on the spread carried patterns. The handles and borders were wrapped in silk fabric. Interestingly, these bamboo fans were very similar in shape to the fans of today. The bamboo strips unearthed at Mawangdui carried the character of "fan," unequivocally proving that fans did exist at that time.

Though the bamboo fans that have been unearthed were first made some 2,000 years ago, they demonstrate rather advanced manufacturing skills. In terms of the materials used, fans in China have been made of feathers, bamboo, silk, and palm leaves. Along with the excavations of more historical sites, fans of even earlier periods may well be discovered. Ancient murals, paintings, and even poems and prose have confirmed the existence of different kinds of fans throughout history.

The fact that the earliest fans were made of bamboo is demonstrated by the poem entitled "Ode to Bamboo Fans" written by Ba

Gu during the Han Dynasty (206 BC-AD 220). In this poem he describes the materials, shapes, and functions of bamboo fans. Xu Xun of the Jin Dynasty (265-420) also wrote a poem praising the superb craft of bamboo fan making, describing the bamboo strips of the fans as being as delicate as cicada wings. The section on the master calligrapher Wang Xizhi, in *The History of Jin*, notes that when Wang ran into an old lady selling a hexagonal-shaped bamboo fan, he wrote five characters on it, which led many people to compete in purchasing it. By the Jin Dynasty, there were already different shaped fans made of different materials.

Silk fans became the carriers of one's sentiment. Round fans were known as "fans of reunion." There have been many stories of love based on these fans, while poems, prose, and inscriptions praising the elegance of the fan have been produced in great numbers.

Carvings on tombstones dating back to the Han Dynasty have expression referring to fans. In a Han tomb in Anqiu County, Shandong Province, which was excavated in the early 1950s, 16 stones with carvings were discovered that portrayed fans in the shape of kitchen choppers. These were on the stones forming the north wall. Murals were popular during the Han Dynasty and three tombs of that period, unearthed in the early 1950s in Liaoyang, reveal murals with round-shaped fans. In 1979, the tomb of Princess Rurulinghe of the Eastern Wei period (534-550), found in Cixian County, Hebei Province, was excavated. The carvings in this tomb, dating from 550, feature seven ladies. The one in the middle, a relatively large figure with a tall hair arrangement, has been described as giving an order with a gesture of her right hand. Apparently this figure was the princess herself. The six other slim figures to her side hold a round fan, a canopy, and cups, indicating they were her servants. The fan depicted has a long handle.

The fan depicted in a mural in the tomb of Princess Xinchengchang, who was the 21st daughter of Emperor Taizong (r. 627-649) of the Tang Dynasty, is the earliest fan seen in a tomb mural. The oblong-shaped fan with a long handle is found in the mural on the east wall of the fifth tunnel in the tomb.

The murals found in the tomb of Princess Yongtai, the 7th daughter of Tang emperor Taizong, also carry images of fans. Princess Yongtai and her husband were killed in 701 by Empress Wu Zetian.

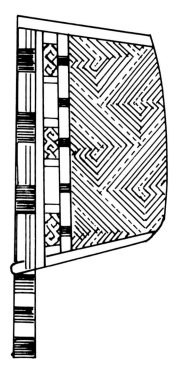

Picture of a bamboo fan dating back to the Warring States Period, unearthed from the N0. 1 tomb at the Mashan Brick Mill, in Hubei.

After the empress lost power in 706, the princess was reburied in the same tomb as her husband. The tomb was painted with many murals and those on the east and west walls in the front chamber show maids holding fans as if they are moving away dust. These round fans have very long handles.

As in the case of Princess Yongtai, her brother Prince Yide (682-701), eldest son of Emperor Zhongzong of the Tang Dynasty, was also killed by Empress Wu. When his father was reinstated, the prince's remains were brought to the family cemetery, known now as the Qianling Mausoleum. His tomb was also decorated with many murals. On the north and west walls of the third tunnel in the tomb there are images of maids holding fans. The fans here are oblong in shape with long handles. These fans directly reflect the shape and size of fans used during that important historical period.

The only real fans of the Tang Dynasty that have been excavated so far are the long-handled round silk fans unearthed from the tomb in Astana in Xinjiang in northwest China. Patterns of birds and flowers were rendered on the fan spread. Zhang Xuan, a painter specializing in drawing figures during the height of the Tang Dynasty, portrayed a lady holding a short-handled round fan in his painting, *Ladies Preparing Newly Woven Silk* (Dao Lian Tu), a copy of which was made later during the Song Dynasty (960-1279) and is now at the Museum of Fine Arts, Boston, in the United States.

Zhou Fang, another Tang Dynasty painter who was noted for his rendering of figures, in *Court Ladies Wearing Flowered Headdresses* (Zan Hua Shi Nu Tu), which is now in the Liaoning Provincial Museum, shows a lady holding a long-handled fan painted with peonies. His painting on silk entitled *Lady Waving a Fan* (Hui Shan Shi Nu Tu), now in the Palace Museum, shows a colored silk spread of the fan. The painting depicts the daily life of palace concubines and maids and portrays thirteen figures. One of them, in a standing position, holds a fan that has a long handle and a spread depicting a pair of birds. *The Seven Wise Men* (Qi Xian Tu), by Tang Dynasty painter Sun Wei, now in the Shanghai Museum, shows a man holding a short-handled fan. In *The Imperial Sedan Chair* (Bu Nian Tu) by Yan Liben, the painter presents Emperor Taizong of the Tang Dynasty sitting on a sedan chair surrounded by nine court ladies either supporting the chair or holding fans and canopies. In another Zhang Xuan painting, *The Empress's Travels* (Huang Hou Xing Xing Tu), the escorts stand in front of or behind the empress holding long-handled fans and canopies.

The Night Revels of Han Xizai (Han Xizai Ye Yan Tu), a masterpiece attributed to Gu Hongzhong of the Five Dynasties (907-960), portrays, in the fourth section, a scene showing Han Xizai enjoying a musical performance. Han is presented as sitting in a chair with a bare chest and holding a fan while listening to music. A maid standing next to him holds a long-handled silk fan decorated with trees and hills. It is shown that the male figures in both *The Seven Wise Men* and *The Night Revels of Han Xizai* are holding short-handled fans with wooden borders. One woman in *Lady Waving a Fan* is using a short-handled fan to tend to the flames in a charcoal stove. Apart from this, other maids and servants always used long-handled fans, as depicted in many murals. The paintings and murals also indicate a transition in the design of fans from an oblong shape to that of a square shape.

2. Fans During the Song Dynasty

$\mathcal{T}$he first fan to appear with calligraphy is believed to be the "fan with the handwriting of Wang Xizhi." Studying the history of painting, however, reveals that scholars and men of letters throughout China's history have left their personal mark on fans. Examples of ancient fans were few in number until the archaeological excavations of Tang Dynasty tombs. For the most part, these fans were often used as simple decoration or purely utilitarian in nature, and were not really considered art objects themselves. By the Song Dynasty, there was an emerging movement of artistically-painted fans. This was due in part to both the establishment of the imperial painting academy as well as the inherent art appreciation system instilled during the previous Five Dynasties period.

The imperial painting academy attracted painters from across the country, especially those from the Western Shu and Southern Tang, two of the states of the Five Dynasties period. During the reign of Emperor Huizong (r. 1068-1085) of the Song, the study of painting was officially incorporated into the imperial examinations in order to bring together painters from all areas of the country. The emperor himself was an avid painter and contributed to the prosperity of the painting academy. Fans became a medium through which artists could express their creative ideas. Out of one hundred paintings collected in the reference work, *Paintings of the Song*, sixty-six were paintings on fans. Small as they were, these paintings covered a great variety of themes and demonstrated a profoundness of meaning, undertaken with meticulous skill. Doing away with the old monotonous style, these paintings created a new category of art in which grand themes and powerful expressions were presented in an unusual but effective format. The imperial examinations—through which the painting academy exerted a significant impact—was a catalyst to the development of the fine arts industry in society. Many scholars who took part in the examinations wrote poems in answer to examination questions con-

A fan-holding maid from a mural found in the tomb of the Tang Dynasty Prince Yide. The tomb, part of the Qianling Mausoleums, is in Qianxian County, Shaanxi Province.

A group of maids seen on a mural in the tomb of Tang Dynasty Princess Yongtai at the Qianling Mausoleums, Qianxian County, Shaanxi Province.

cerning the art depicted on fans. Some of these poems have become long-lasting lines that have been passed down for generations.

These poetic expressions and commentaries broadened the ideas of creativity, and opened a new chapter in the art of fan painting. The withering flowers, drifting clouds, gurgling streams, peaceful trees, and howling winds all found their way onto fan paintings. After this, fans became like stories, poems, and musical journeys in providing people with excitement and vigor in generating their thoughts, and in expanding their imagination. The fans brought them joy and mesmerized them.

Ladies Preparing Newly Woven Silk (Dao Lian Tu), segment of a painting by Zhang Xuan of the Tang Dynasty.

3. The Rise of Folding Fans

$\mathcal{A}$s tools for keeping people cool, fans had been available both in China and in other parts of the world for a long time. Along with the cultural and economic exchanges between East and West, a different kind of fan, the folding fan, began to appear in China. The first folding fan arrived as a tribute that was brought to China by a Japanese monk in 988. Writings of both Japanese and Chinese scholars concerning the folding fan, which was believed to have been first invented in Japan, apparently suggest that it received its shape from the design of a bat 's wing. According to Guo Ruoxu, when Korean envoys came to China, they also brought folding fans as gifts. Their folding fans employed light blue paper for the spread, and they were painted with exquisite portraitures of Korean nobility, ladies, horses, riverside scenery, lotus, flowers, and water birds. The clouds, moon, and sun patterns rendered on these fans were extremely attractive.

Lady Waving a Fan (Hui Shan Shi Nu Tu), segment of a painting by Zhou Fang of the Tang Dynasty.

The Imperial Sedan Chair (Bu Nian Tu), segment of a painting by Yan Liben of the Tang Dynasty.

Court Ladies Wearing Flowered Headdresses (Zan Hua Shi Nu Tu), segment of a painting by Zhou Fang of the Tang Dynasty.

Night Revels of Han Xizai (Han Xizai Ye Yan Tu), segment of a painting by Gu Hongzhong of the Five Dynasties.

The Chinese referred to the fans as Japanese fans since it was Japan where they were first made. Zhang Shinan wrote in his book, *Travel Stories*, that an envoy from Korea brought three boxes of pinefans and two folding fans. It can be inferred from this that folding fans were not only introduced to China from Japan but also from Korea. Folding fans as tributes and gifts from Japan and Korea came into the Northern Song Dynasty (960-1127) and gradually became popular in China. Writers of the Southern Song Dynasty (1127-1279) recorded the names of folding fan makers and sellers, indicating that folding fans were already in fashion in China.

While folding fans from Japan and Korea grew in popularity in China, the traditional silk round fans remained in the mainstream during the Song Dynasty. As a result of the special favoritism for paintings demonstrated by the Song court, round fans with paintings became quite popular. Handicraft fans were no less popular. Lacquer fans, in particular, were among the unique handicrafts during the Song Dynasty. A pair of lacquer fans with open-work turning handles were unearthed from the tomb of Zhou Yu of the Southern Song Dynasty, and can be described as lacquer craft of superb workmanship. One of the fans features a wooden handle. The cover was made by pasting paper on thin bamboo strip frames as thin as a human hair. The border of the fan was rendered in black lacquer, while the fan cover was painted with a dense dark red cloud pattern. The handle was connected to the cover through the crescent holder of the fan cover, which was 10 inches long and 8 inches wide, whereas the handle was 6 inches long and 5/8 inch thick in diameter. The other fan had the same kind of fan cover, but its handle had three groups of open-work sculptures that could be rotated.

The excavation of the tomb of Huang Sheng in the northern suburbs of Fuzhou, also dating back to the Southern Song Dynasty, yielded a round fan. The excavation report said that the fan "was by the right hand of the deceased". When unearthed, the fan still retained the patterns of one pink peach blossom and fragments of two to three leaves. The black lacquer on the handle and the frame of the fan had fallen away. The handle had been polished while the cover was made of palm fiber. The entire fan cover was 5 3/4 inches long and 5-7 1/4 inches wide. This demonstrates that the Song Dynasty had its own traditional culture in terms of the type of fans, though folding fans that had been introduced from Japan and Korea were already being made in China. At this time folding fans were not as popular.. In *Cooling off Under the Willow Shade* (Liu Yin Fo Shu Tu) on the lacquer box from the No. 5 tomb of the Southern Song Dynasty in Cunqian Township, Wujin County of Changzhou, two ladies are portrayed, one holding a round fan and the other a folding fan. The frame of the folding fan can be clearly seen. This was the earliest portrayal of a folding fan seen to date, indicating that round and folding fans co-existed during the Song Dynasty. The work also served to reinforce the notion that a new object can be accepted by the public if its practicality and convenience of use has universal appeal.

Though folding fans emerged and were produced during the Song Dynasty, they were met with some resistance because some people believed they were intended for the lower social classes. According to *Random Notes of the Spring Breeze Hall* by Lu Shen of the Ming Dynasty (1368-1644), envoys from the southeast region during the early Ming were laughed at because they held folding fans. Gao Shiqi, an author of the Qing Dynasty (1644-1911), also noted that folding fans were used by servants who hid them in their sleeves. On the whole, folding

Clearing Up After a Snowfall (Xue Ji Tu), painting done during the Song Dynasty.

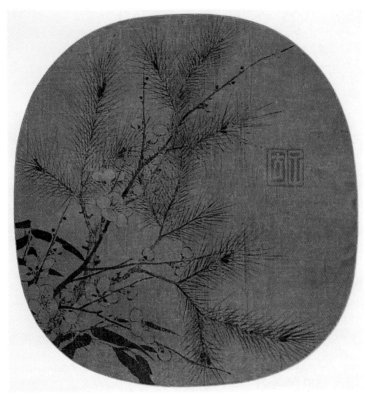

Three Friends in Winter time (Sui Han San You Tu) by Zhao Mengjian of the Southern Song Dynasty.

Left Top: A Mountain View in the Rain (Xi Shan Feng Yu Tu), painting from the Song Dynasty.
Left Bottom: Going Home After Drinking (Hua Wu Zui Gui Tu), painting from the Song Dynasty.

fans were rare before the Ming Dynasty, which has led people to state that folding fans began to appear during the time of Emperor Yongle whose reign lasted from 1403 to 1424. It was Emperor Yongle who showed a great interest in folding fans, ushering in a period of popularity for this latecomer to the fan family. Emperor Yongle gave folding fans to his ministers and generals as highly valued gifts, thus helping to spread the popularity of such fans among the populace. Liu Yuanqing wrote that ladies in south China used round fans, while only prostitutes favored folding fans. He continued to suggest that in more recent years this custom was quickly changing as women of good reputation also began to use folding fans. For folding fans to gain favor first in the imperial court and then to find their way to the common people certainly took time.

Excavation results suggest that most of the folding fans of the Ming Dynasty belonged to the middle and later periods. The producers were largely confined to Sichuan and Suzhou. In his book on products from the country, Xie Zhaozhi of the Ming Dynasty noted that "Fans from Sichuan and Suzhou were most popular whether at the imperial court or among ordinary people. Each year, over a million fans from Sichuan went to the imperial court as tribute and were used by the very top and middle-level court officials. Each fan was worth one tael of gold." *The Annual of Yedi* recorded: "During the Ming Dynasty, fans from Sichuan were considered superior. The government of Sichuan gave 11,540 fans to the imperial court. During the year 1551, under the reign of Emperor Jiajing of the Ming, an additional 2,100 fans were ordered by the emperor to give away as gifts. In 1564, another 800 small-sized delicate fans were ordered for the emperor's concubines." From this we can infer that women at that time used smaller-sized, delicate fans. The same author also described the fans used by women as carrying images of a dragon on the front, the side, and in groups of a hundred, as well as patterns of birds.

Wen Zhenheng of the Ming Dynasty wrote in his book on the variety of utensils that "fans made by the government of Sichuan for the imperial court were the most expensive, as they were made with gilded frames and extremely thin silk." He went on to say that "Suzhou was most famous for its fans with paintings and calligraphy on them. Their frames were built with white bamboo, brown bamboo, black hard wood, sandalwood, etc. Occasionally ivory and hawksbill turtle bones were used. The fan spreads were mostly white or gilded so that the owners could ask established calligraphers and painters to render their works on them. Such fans could be priceless." Wen wrote that people did not want to use fans with fine calligraphy or paintings on them, but rather kept them in boxes to be admired as art objects. In time it had become a custom for the people of Suzhou to collect artistic fans, thus making Suzhou fans less practical than those from Sichuan. According to Wen, fans from Sichuan served a clearly practical purpose while those from Suzhou held artistic value.

Xie Zhaozhi of the Ming Dynasty wrote that gilded fans from Suzhou were the most expensive. Artists from Suzhou created a large quantity of fans depicting traditional Chinese paintings, and they combined poetry, calligraphy, and painting on the fan spread. A great number of experienced artisans crafting fan frames and spreads had now emerged. In addition, fans from Nanjing and Hangzhou also gained notoriety. By the middle and late Ming Dynasty, folding fans had become the fashion of the day and threatened the continued production of round fans.

4. Fans in Arts and Crafts

$\mathcal{F}$ans have developed over the course of history, with their makers absorbing and learning from each other so as to give rise to two major schools: those of the round fans and those of the folding fans. Upon the vast landscape of China and among its huge population, however, there were many varieties of fans that were equally charming, demonstrating the diligence and wisdom of the people. In terms of industrial arts, woven bamboo, vines, palm leaves, and even ivory were all materials used in the making of fans. Lacquer and carving techniques were all applied to fan making. Fans made of feathers are another example in this great category. Feather fans dating back to the Spring and Autumn and Warring States periods have been unearthed in Hubei Province. During the Han Dynasty, feather fans were quite popular in eastern China. Feather fans from Gaochun in Jiangsu Province—with a history of more than 500 years—were known for their elegance and graceful look. Ordinary feather fans were made of goose feathers, while expensive fans used the feathers of cranes, swans, and falcons.

Palm-leaf fans also have a long history, as they grew to popularity during the Wei and Jin dynasties (220-420). Palm-leaf fans with patterns burned on them by fire once carried a great reputation. They have been found in Xinhui of Guangdong Province, a place known as a hometown of many thousands of overseas Chinese. Such fans were bought by local people in Guangdong and were seen in mountain villages and by fishing ponds. The palm leaves for making the fans originated in Xinhui. The tender white leaves with fine grains and no cracks were considered the choicest of materials. Gauze of yellow, green, or white was often used to wrap the edges of the palm leaves. The handles were often burned with patterns, or carved with calligraphy or painted patterns. The most expensive palm-leaf fans were gilded.

Fragrant sandalwood fans came into being as folding fans. It is said that Suzhou produced the first sandalwood fan in 1920 in a workshop called Zhangs' Factory. Around 1930, Wang Xing's Fan Store, a shop in Hangzhou well-known for selling fans, commissioned a Suzhou fan factory to produce sandalwood fans according to samples of imported Japanese fans, which were the favorite of the market at that time. Later, these sandalwood fans became brand-name items for Wang

Landscape painting on a fan by Ni Yunlu.

Xing's Fan Store. They were named for scenic sites in Hangzhou, such as the Jade Belt and the Twin Pagodas.

Sandalwood fans were manufactured in great varieties and their frames vary from wide to narrow and short to long. Pieces of wide fan frames, burned, carved, inlaid, or painted with patterns, are put together to create the fan spread. Silk is also used in making the spread.

Ivory fans in particular are an exquisite (and expensive) variation on the art. There were also many other kinds of art and craft fans made, including the black paper fans at Wang Xing's Fan Store in Hangzhou; the bamboo-silk fans made by Gong Yuzhang, known as a master of fan making. Gong's fans have earned the title "Number 1 fans on earth" with a gold folding fan only one inch wide, with its spread supported by a 13-piece frame gilded with 18-karat gold. It is only 0.2 millimeters thick.

The culture of Chinese fans is a profound topic for further study, while the development of fans reflects the wisdom of the Chinese people. Small as they are, fans have defined the most outstanding achievements in arts and crafts throughout the centuries. They also accentuate the expressiveness and creativity of the traditional Chinese arts of calligraphy and painting. Fans also demonstrate the absorption of foreign influences and adaptation of popular culture, which have become an inseparable part of its history.

Landscape in Imitation of the Work of Huang Zijiu, painted on a fan by Wang Yuanqi.

5. Handled Fans

*A*lthough fans come in a multitude of different styles and forms, there are basically two categories of fans: handled fans and folding fans.

The earliest examples of handled fans discovered to date was a short-handled woven bamboo fan of the Spring and Autumn and Warring States period unearthed in Jiangling, Hubei Province, in 1982. This type of fan was made by attaching a handle to the lower bottom of the fan spread. In order to fasten the two parts so as to make the fan structurally solid, a holder is fixed between the fan spread and the handle. For expensive fans, decorative objects were also attached to the handle.

The long history of fans has allowed many varieties of handled fans to be made using a diverse selection of materials and with different qualities and characteristics. Apart from serving the purpose of keeping the fan owner cool, fans also reflected the social status of the owners, such as those fixed to carriages or held by servants.

The popularity of handled can be attributed to their diverse forms and uses. They were crafted of bamboo, feather, paper, palm-leaf, ivory, and silk. Among bamboo fans, there were those woven of bamboo strips and those made of bamboo threads sometimes as thin as a hair. Feather fans included those made of white goose feathers, crane feathers, magpie feathers, hawk feathers, and pheasant feathers. Paper fans were composed of oilpaper and bamboo paper for their spreads. There were also fans made from paper-cuts pasted on gilded paper. Ivory fans included those whose spread was made with thin strips of ivory joined together, and silk fans were made of different types of silk material.

In terms of their shapes, handled fans included round, oblong, hexagonal, octagonal, as well as gourds, crab apples, hearts, diamonds, sunflowers, jade pendants, palace lanterns, and bells. The round silk fans were the most popular variety of handled fans and have been extolled in more literary works than any other fan shapes. Ban Jie, an author of the Han Dynasty, compared round silk fans to the roundness of the moon. As for silk fans, those made of silk gauze and thin, tough silk were often the most popular. Silk fans, however, were banned during the Eastern Jin Dynasty in the 5th century, because they were used as objects associated with gambling. The earliest silk fans known to date is a wooden-handled fan unearthed in 1973 from a Tang Dynasty tomb at Astana, Turpan, Xinjiang. The round silk fan spread is 5.3 inches in diameter and painted with a pair of birds holding flowers in their bills. At the top are decorations of flowers while at the bottom there is scenery depicting a mountain.

During the Song Dynasty, an imperial art academy was established, and a large contingent of artists used fans as the media onto which they expressed themselves artistically. Painted fans of the Song Dynasty helped write one of the most brilliant chapters in the history

Sandalwood fan (Wang Xing's Fan Store).

Top: Black silk fan (Wang Xing's Fan Store).
Bottom: Facial masks (Wang Xing's Fan Store).

Top: Painted cloth fan (Wang Xing's Fan Store).
Bottom: Folding fan with a landscape painting (Wang Xing's Fan Store).

of traditional painting in China. During the Ming and Qing dynasties, fans with silk on both sides were favored, and colors such as celadon, muddy gold, and lake water, were introduced. The fan spread was mostly made with refined silk which was both thin yet strong. The patterns on the fan spread were rendered by such techniques as painting, *kesi* (fine silk and gold thread) weaving, embroidery, pasting, and drawing. Fan making attracted many skilled artisans, many of whom were experts in their respective fields. Many of the fans became objects of art, preserved and treasured in private collections.

Fans unearthed from tombs dating back to the Warring States Period, and Western Han, Tang, and Song dynasties, can be seen on the murals of the Eastern Wei and early Tang dynasties. These fans had both long and short handles. Fans portrayed by Yan Liben of the Tang Dynasty in his *Imperial Sedan Chair* as well as Zhang Xuan in *The Empress's Travels*, all featured long handles—twice as long than the fan spread. The wooden-handled silk fan excavated from the Tang tomb at Astana of Turpan, Xinjiang, also has a handle more than twice as long as the diameter of the fan spread. This indicates that the length of the handle was not entirely dictated by the ratio between the diameter of the fan spread and the length of the handle. Those who held long handled fans were probably servants such as court maids and servants.

A study of the materials used for making fan handles includes a bamboo fan unearthed from the Mashan tomb in Jiangling, Hubei, which dates to the Warring States Period that had a bamboo handle, as did a fan excavated from the Mawangdui tomb in Changshan. A silk fan from the Astana tomb in Turpan, Xinjiang, of the Tang Dynasty, had a wooden handle. Another fan with a wooden handle was found in Huang Sheng's tomb in the northern suburbs of Fuzhou. It dates to the Southern Song Dynasty and has indications which tell us that it was processed with a grinding wheel, while one of the round fans from Zhou Yu 's tomb in Jintan, also belonging to the Southern Song Dynasty, had a very long wooden handle. Interestingly, another fan from the same tomb had a carved open-work revolving handle coated with lacquer. The open-work carving actually consisted of three designs, carrying symmetrical patterns of clouds revolving around a central axis. These artifacts have provided us with insight into the materials used for handles during the Warring States Period, and subsequent Han, Tang, and Song dynasties.

The round fan unearthed from the tomb of Zhou Yu in Jintan, dating from the Southern Song Dynasty, had a crescent-shaped holder on the handle to support the fan spread. Typically, all the expensive fans had such holders, which could be in a "Y" shape, clipping the fan spread. The holder could also be in the shape of a traditional Chinese "good wishes" objects, such as the shape of a peach. The holder did not actually protect the fan spread but mainly served the purpose of decoration, adding overall beauty to the entire fan.

While the handles were often crafted of fine wood, the ends of the handles—sometimes called the butt of the fan—were usually inlaid with gold or silver either in dots or with threads. For such objects, the handle butts were also inlaid with green jade, ruby, sapphire, white jade, and agate.

6. Folding Fans and Their Characteristics

*F*olding fans are comprised of two parts: the spread and the frame. In addition there are ancillary parts such as fasteners, or nails and tassels or pendants. The overall spread consists of the main spread and the border. The central strips forming the frame tend to be wide, while the two thick strips at both ends are referred to as "backbones." The central strips are known as "small bones." The length of the backbones are usually within a distance of 12 inches, while the "small bones" are usually comprised of an odd number of parts. In situations where the "small bones" are in even numbers, they are usually comprised of 16 pieces, yet are still the same overall length as fans with an odd-number of small bones. When the length is comprised of a full foot, the bones can be grouped in either even or odd numbers. The part of the small bones that are wrapped by the fan spread are called "heart tips," while the lower part of the bones below the fastening nail is referred to as the fan butt. For the two side backbones, these are known from section to section, as the "top bone," "shoulder," "lower bone," and "butt."

Fan spreads are divided into colored and white, which are commonly referred to simply as "plain." Among the colored spreads, gold is generally the most highly valued.

To produce a gold spread, gold foil or gold powder, mixed with glue, was turned into "gold paste," which was then painted on white fan spreads to create the effect of a golden finish. According to historical documents, in making gold paste a person used one finger to dip into glue in order to capture the gold foil and put it on a plate. The person used another finger to grind and roll it into paste. There are also records indicating that the craftsman's right palm was used to grind and roll the gold foil into paste.

Gold paste began to be applied to fan spreads at a very early time, as products utilizing gold paste first appeared during the Tang Dynasty. To make gold paste fan spreads, gold foil was produced from actual gold. According to the *Almanac of Wuxian County*, gold foil made in Suzhou was one inch long on each side, and each tael of gold could produce 2,319 pieces of gold foil. The gold foil could be any of the three shades: "dachi," a robust gold color, which maintained the origi-

Southern Song Dynasty round fan unearthed from the tomb of Zhou Yu in Jintan.

Sketch of a round fan (fan spread, fan border, fan holder, fan handle, fan butt).

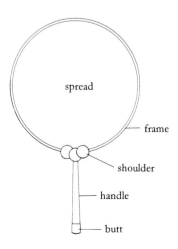

spread

frame

shoulder

handle

butt

nal color of the gold; "fochi," or Buddha gold color, which was a dark golden shade with red copper mixed in; and "tianchi," or field gold, which contained silver threads and carried a light golden hue. The gold foil used to make gold paste could be in any of these three colors. It had to be crushed in order to produce very refined gold paste. Nowadays the replacement of gold powder produced by special technology is often applied to products where gold paste was previously used.

Thrown gold, mottled gold, and cold gold, were products made by slightly different methods of processing. To create their effect, glue was first applied to the fan spread, then small pieces of gold foil

Seven Sages (Qi Xian Tu) by Sun Wei of the Tang Dynasty.

were sprinkled onto the glue like snowflakes. The result is referred to as spotted gold. If the fan spread was rendered with large patches, the result is known as thrown gold. If the entire fan spread was covered with gold foil, the result is called cold gold. Some fan producers described their fans, which had cold gold on one side and plain white paper on the other as semi-cold gold fans. In all these processing methods gold foil of varied shades could be applied. The actual production of fans, however, was not as simple as it may sound. Individual fan makers, for example, always retained their own unique techniques and different materials for producing special fans for special clients. Different fan makers used different terms for some of the techniques, especially for some of their unique characteristics of ways of manufacture.

Throughout history most of the well-known artists designated specific fan-making workshops for their needs, so that they remained well-practiced and well-versed in the art of fan painting. Of the fans dating to the Ming Dynasty that have so far been unearthed, most had a gold paste finish. The amount of gold applied on a fan spread reflected the wealth and social status of its owner, to the delight of scholars and officials, as well as to collectors.

Apart from the gold paste finish, there were other types of fan spreads with varied shades of black, blue, green, and red. Unfortunately most of these varieties have been lost.

Plain white fan spreads, made of materials varying from paper to silk, have always been the predominant type of fan spreads. Those made of paper were not only greater in quantity and variety but were also the first to emerge and be produced on a large scale. Made using a complicated process, they were usually comprised of three to five layers of Chinese painting paper. In some cases, top quality painting paper was used for the surface finish on both sides, with cotton fiber and bamboo paper in between.

Not only was the material important to the fan spread, the manufacturing process was equally significant. Though all in plain white color, fan spreads could have qualities that were widely differentiated. Quality paper ensured ease in moving a paint brush smoothly as well as a kind of elasticity that endured over time. Making a fan could require ten processes including choosing the materials, polishing, cutting, mounting, brushing, folding, and bordering.

Also worth mentioning was the unusual "three-section fan spread," made especially for explicit or pornographic pictures. Upon opening the fan to the left, the pornographic picture would be revealed, while opening it to the right would reveal an altogether different, non-pornographic picture as a cover up.

Folding fan frames, which are classically beautiful and elegant, embody the most profound aspects of culture. They are made of expensive and unique materials and carry a plainly elegant decorative quality, pleasing to the eye. They instill imagination in terms of workmanship, and richly complement the fan spreads to constitute a relationship known as "green leaves and red blossoms enhancing the beauty of each other."

The materials for making fan frames come from a wide range of sources, including sandalwood, ivory, and black hard wood that were considered to be ordinary materials during the Ming Dynasty, while bamboo was regarded as an elegant material. The fans made in Suzhou over the years that emphasized the painting and calligraphy on the fan spreads made use of white bamboo, brown bamboo, black hard wood, and sandalwood for their vanes and frames. Occasionally ivory was also used as a material for fan frames.

The choice of materials for making fan frames was of the uppermost importance. The next important factors are the processes that are used, which include polishing, applying lacquer, carving, and inlaying. In the case of bamboo, there are also the processes of selecting, boiling, drying, piercing, shaping, and baking before any polishing of the frames can begin. Hard wood, ivory, animal bones, and animal horns also need to be polished before any lacquer is applied.

As for polishing, water produces a special effect, particularly in the case of the types of bamboo which have unusual, natural qualities, such as spotted bamboo with colorful grains and dots that look even more shiny and crystalline after polishing with water. Lacquer, on the other hand, helps make up for inadequacies inherent in certain materials. If polishing enhances the natural beauty of the bamboo, then applying lacquer is a process of artificial beautification. Lacquering, which became popular during the Ming Dynasty, can be applied in a variety of ways such as single-color lacquering and spotted lacquering. Of these, the starry, red-coral lacquer, golden raindrops, and snowflakes have been the most popular. The former uses red-coral lacquer as a background with small silvery flakes smoked into yellow thrown onto it. The latter also uses red-coral lacquer as the background but with gold flakes thrown on it. There is also a wide variety of the so-called eight-treasure lacquers. For the most part, flowery patterns are applied to the backbones of such frames leaving the border of the backbones for further decoration. Lacquering ensures a shiny finish to the backbones with colorful patterns without loosing the quality of elegance.

Carving is a decorating process for the frame bones. There are

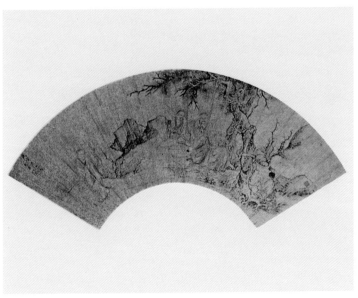

A Gathering of Men of Letters (Wen Hui Tu) by You Qiu of the Ming Dynasty.

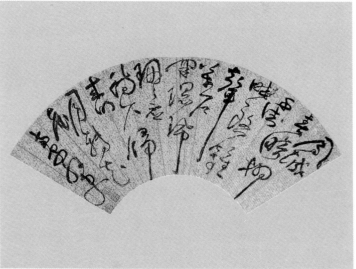

Top: The Beginning of Spring (Chun Xiao Tu) by Sun Yi of the Qing Dynasty.
Bottom: Calligraphy in cursive script by Feng Fang of the Ming Dynasty.

many themes used in the carving process, but meticulous workmanship is the key. Carving on bamboo reflects the effectiveness of the technique in bringing out the differences in the depth of carving, especially when some of the original green skin of the bamboo is left untouched so as to create a special effect. When some of the bamboo skin is left to serve as grains, this creates a beautiful contrast of colors next to the carved part that reveals the yellowish inside portion of the bamboo.

There are also other processes such as bordering, wrapping, inlaying, and firing to beautify the different kinds of materials for fan frames. In the case of animal bones, inlaying and firing can be applied. Lacquered bones can be carved or painted. These processes open up possibilities for interesting creations and endless themes.

Structurally speaking, fan frames are relatively simple, but their shoulders and butts provide great room for variation. The length, width, number of bones, and shape of the bones of the frames determine the shape of the fans. Of these, the variation of the shoulders and the number of bones are the most important factors. Fan shoulders are often found in the lower part of the backbones. However, if they are placed at the middle, they are referred to as the contrasting shoulders, while if they are in the upper part, they are known as reversed shoulders. Fan butts can come in many shapes, including swallow tail, magnolia, plum blossom, and bamboo joints, but those most often seen are either round or square. Backbones are classified into plain and painted categories, and are of varying widths. The painted backbones are usually straight and smooth while the plain backbones are usually curved.

Folding fans used by men are mostly 12 inches long with 16 or 18 bones, while those used by women are smaller in size, usually only 8 inches long.

Fan butts are one of the most charming and special aspects of folding fans. The city of Suzhou, for instance, is famous for collecting examples of fan butts, which have been very popular in folk arts and crafts. Suzhou is also famous for the great number of experienced fan frame makers who were active during the 1950s and 1960s. Some of the fan butts first used during the Ming Dynasty were later used with new fan spreads during the Qing Dynasty and the Republican period early in the 20th century.

Fan nails, small as they are, are extremely important to every fan. First, a hole is drilled into the bones, then an ox horn nail is driven into the hole, and finally a cap is added by firing. To fire a cap is by no means easy. Normally, "pincer firing" and "drill firing" are the methods used. These not only prevent the nails from falling out but also create the effect of a "mouse eye," commonly known as "a grain of pepper." Some fan makers even add a nail cover on top of the "mouse eye."

In order to further beautify the fan butts, some makers have put jade, gold, silver, and copper strips as well as other colorful materials in the shape of rings, diamonds, and other inlaid patterns into the fan backbones. Then nails are fired onto the top of these decorations. The nail covers and the inlaid decorations complement one another.

7. The Art of Fan Painting

*A*ccording to historical documents, Wang Xizhi, the great artist of the Eastern Jin Dynasty, is known as the first artist to paint on a round silk fan. Painted fans dating back to the Tang Dynasty have been unearthed. These paintings on fans reflect some of the original paintings handed down through history. By the time of the Song Dynasty, the development of this type of painting created a close relationship between men of letters and artists, leading to a new class of art appealing to the literati. Furthermore, the special favor shown toward fan paintings by the emperor gave a great impetus to the development of this art, which at the time reached its highest level.

The art of fan painting flourished during the Song Dynasty and has left us with a rich body of long lasting artwork demonstrating the superb craft of workmanship of the artists of that period while shedding light on some of the most outstanding traditions in the history of Chinese painting. Even small images of wild grass and flowers, insects, birds, and fish in these "flower and bird paintings" are all meticulously executed with extreme care. Large-size landscape paintings brought out the loftiness and magnificence of mountains. A method of painting objects in wrinkles was employed to vividly por-

Evolution of Fan Types

No.	Era		Type	Diagram
1	Yuan		round	
2	Ming Dynasty	Early Ming	magnolia	
3			swallow tail	
4			stirrup square	
5			eggplant	
6			big round	
7			water chestnut	
8			flat round	
9		Mid-Ming	classic square	
10			classic round	
11			classic small square	
12		Late	thin stirrup	
13			drum round	
14	Qing Dynasty	Early Qing	eggplant	
15			small rice	
16			horse tooth	
17			horse tooth-accordion	
18			small flower vase	
19			big flower vase	
20			big round fan	
21			small round fan	
22			straight gourd round	
23		Mid-Qing	row of eggplant	
24			straight eggplant	
25			stirrup	
26			inverted wheel	

No.	Era		Type	Diagram
27	Qing Dynasty	Mid-Qing	round gourd	
28			palm fan	
29			inverted wheel square	
30		Late Qing	flat bamboo joint	
31			square bamboo root	
32			round pipa	
33			small chestnut round	
34	Since 1912		square accordion	
35			thin onion	
36			bamboo root	
37			butterfly	
38			holed bottle	
39			big hook	
40			three-section bottle	
41			olive	
42			gold fish	
43			small hook	
44			pine branch	
45			open shoulder eggplant	
46			electric bulb	
47			water caltrop	
48			nail into gourd round	
49			gingko fruit	
50			small twin coin	
51			duck egg round	
52			plum round	
53			double drum round	
54			octagonal round	
55			small semi-circle round	
56			fish eye round	
57			round drum	

tray the miraculously changing mountains, rolling hills, mists, clouds, rain, and snow, in panoramic views. During the Southern Song period, partial-scenery paintings came into fashion and gave prominence to portraying detail, rather than depicting the overall view. This development made the composition of these paintings simpler and the themes they presented more emphatic in order to produce a complete effect in the imagination of the viewer.

Portraits during the Song Dynasty demonstrated a high-level of artistic progress. They were more expressive in presenting the feelings and sentiments of those portrayed. *Tending Horse by the Willow Pond* (Liu Tang Mu Ma Tu) by Chen Juzhong, for example, portrayed over 20 people and more than 50 horses, each of which differed from the others in expression.

The paintings on fans during this period were an important component of the history of painting of the Song Dynasty. In fact they

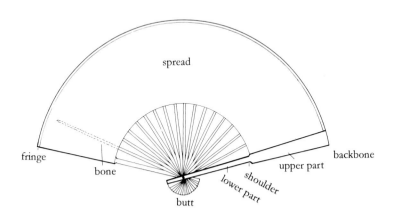

Sketch of a folding fan.

can be described as the pinnacle of Song Dynasty paintings. Small as they were, they vividly reflected the larger world. As an art form that had been carried on for a long time, fan paintings had changed fans from their traditional practical role as tools for keeping people cool into genuine objects of art. Paintings on silk fans also had become collectors ' items among members of the royal family, the nobility, as well as prominent scholars. Many of the fan paintings from the Yuan

White-headed Birds in a Bamboo Grove (Bai Tou Cong Zhu Tu) done during the Song Dynasty.

Dynasty (1271-1368), including the *Yueyang Tower* (Yue Yang Low Tu) by Xia Yong, and *Tree and Rock* (Shu Shi Tu), by Zhao Yuan, are excellent examples. During the Ming and Qing dynasties, there were also many artists enthusiastic about fan painting, and fans remain favored art objects to this day. The varied shapes of the fans added to the beauty of the fan paintings. Painted silk fans were particularly favored

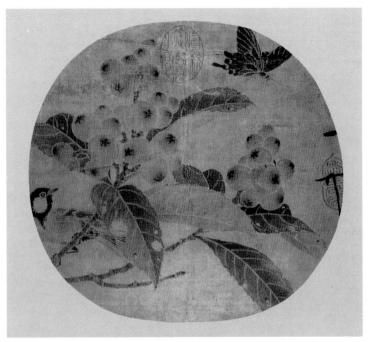

Bird in Loquat Tree (Pi Pa Shan Niao Tu) by Zhao Ji of the Northern Song Dynasty.

by collectors because of their small size and convenience for safe-keeping. Painted fans from the Song and Yuan dynasties are collected not only by large museums in China, but also by museums around the world.

Painted folding fans also first appeared during the Song Dynasty. The most impressive folding fan painting that can still be seen today is the large folding fan painted in 1427 during the Ming Dynasty, now kept in the Palace Museum in Beijing. A work known as

Top: Wagtail by the Lotus Pond (He Tang Ji Ling Tu) done during the Song Dynasty.
Bottom: Lotus in Bloom (Chu Shui Fu Rong Tu) done during the Song Dynasty.

The Dingshu Fishing Boat (Ding Shu Diao Yuan Tu), was painted on a fan by Xie Jin, who was active during the early 15th century. It is kept in the Shanghai Museum and is the earliest folding fan painting still extant today. The position stated by Gao Shiqi of the Qing Dynasty that folding fan painting came into fashion in the Chenghua period (r. 1465-87) of the Ming Dynasty has its roots in the social customs of the time. Wen Zhenheng of the Ming Dynasty once wrote that "People in Suzhou most valued painted fans." They bought fans either plain in color or with gold background and then asked famous calligraphers or artists to paint or write on them. This practice, according to Wen, was in great fashion at the time. Suzhou during that period was experiencing a prosperous economy. At the same time, the original school of palace painters was gradually losing its influence. Instead, the Wumen school, represented by four artists: Shen Zhou, Wen Zhiming, Tang Yin, and Qiu Ying, was gaining popularity. The Wumen school possessed a mature painting technique and its characteristic themes covered a wide range of subjects. Active from the early 15th century to the early 16th century, these artists marked the most dynamic period of calligraphy and painting during the Ming Dynasty. Many of their works that have been handed down through the years were masterpieces rendered on fans. Thanks to their efforts, paintings on folding fans became a pursuit not only for established artists, but also for the nobility and scholars, culminating in the unique painting form with its special charm.

The clever composition of paintings on fans could give people the impression that they were looking at a long rectangular painting on a flat piece of paper, rather than something confined to a semi-circular fan spread. In a way, the illustrations on folding fans were more reflective of the real skill of each calligrapher or artist than were his actual paintings on flat paper! Precisely because of this feature, calligraphers and artists were eager to demonstrate their level of artistic attainment on fans, and they left behind a large number of such masterpieces. Many scholars have studied and written about the composition of paintings on fans, believing that landscapes are characterized by the following: first, the paintings stretch across the entire fan spread; second, even the edges and borders of the fan spread have been considered in the composition; and third, a common theme is to present views of both banks of a river. For most of the fan spread paintings of flowers, birds and, portraits, there are two ways of judging the elements. One is to concentrate on and radiate from the central axis of the surface to be painted, and the other is to focus on the borders and edges. For calligraphy, a typical manner is to keep the characters wide at the top and narrow at the bottom and to arrange the space on the fan spread in accordance with the exact number of characters.

Like all media in which development embodies maintaining existing traditions while developing new ideas, the art of painting during the Ming and Qing dynasties saw the emergence of different schools of art and the rise of many gifted and talented artists. Paintings on

Pine Peak Tower (Song Feng Lou Guan Tu) done during the Song Dynasty.

Top: Silktree (Ye He Hua Tu) done during the Song Dynasty.
Bottom: Peach Blossoms (Bi Tao Tu) done during the Song Dynasty.

Top: Myna on an Aged Tree (Ku Shu Qu Yu Tu) done during the Song Dynasty.
Bottom: Camellia and Butterfly (Cha Hua Hu Die Tu) done during the Song Dynasty.

fans was now part of the Chinese canon of painting which gave expression to the artistic features and splendor of each artist of every school. The uniqueness of fan spreads greatly aroused the curiosity of artists who eagerly rendered their works of painting and calligraphy on them, eventually taking fans to a great artistic height. Painted folding fans of the Ming and Qing dynasties thus marked another milestone in the art of creating fan spreads.

The success of painting on fans lay in the harmonious unity of composition, layout, color, lines, and images. The colors on folding fan paintings were another step forward in the art of painting. Indeed, to put colors on backgrounds of gold paste, mottled gold, gold flakes, and other backgrounds was quite different from working on plain white paper and silk. These background colors were not allowed to contradict the colors of the paintings, which made painting difficult. Those who succeeded in doing paintings on colored fan spreads were able to use gold or other colors to set off their paintings with dark or green lines so as to achieve an effect of striking nobility and polished finish.

Lines cannot be detached from the overall composition and layout. This is true whether the watercolor painter uses bold lines, meticulously executed themes, or simple sketches and drawings. Any carelessness will result in failure for the entire work.

Paintings on fans are varied, from several simple lines in the case of painting bamboo or orchids to meticulous and complex paintings of panoramic views embodying towers, terraces, and pavilions. Experienced connoisseurs, after unfolding a painted fan, will first make an appraisal of the work from the image depicted on the fan spread, examining such factors as the spirit, mood, and skill of the painting so as to fully understand the artist's layout, composition, and the artist's skill with the brush. From the artist's use of colors, the connoisseur will try to judge the characteristics of his painting, as well as the style to which it belongs.

In general, the Ming and Qing dynasties saw the emergence of many well-established artists whose works have become masterpieces of their time and are still appreciated many centuries later. Many museums in China each have a collection of up to a thousand pieces. Even the Suzhou Museum has some one thousand painted fans.

8. Noted Figures and Famous Painted Fans

𝒟uring the Northern Song Dynasty, Emperor Huizong was personally very interested in doing paintings on fan spreads, which soon increased the value of painted fans. He also set an example for many to follow in later times. It can be said that it was under the personal advocacy of emperors that painted fans came into fashion and gained great headway. This naturally led to the emergence of noted artists associated with famous painted fans. Fans containing the calligraphy of emperors, paintings by prime ministers or senior court ministers, and works by scholars who excelled in the imperial examinations became items sought by collectors. These fans not only had authors of high social position, but the art they depicted was of great social and artistic merit. The paintings by Emperor Huizong and the calligraphy in his style, for example, were considered works of extremely high artistic attainment.

The fan entitled *Bird and Loquat Tree* (Pi Pa Shan Niao Tu), created by Emperor Huizong, is now kept in the Palace Museum in Beijing and has been described in many books. Emperor Huizong (1082-1135), whose real name was Zhao Ji, was the last emperor of the Northern Song Dynasty. A fatuous and incompetent ruler, he nevertheless was an extremely capable artist. In his time the royal painting institute became quite prominent and the study of paintings was incorporated into the imperial examinations. It was a period in which palace paintings enjoyed their highest popularity in history. The watercolor paintings created by the emperor which depicted birds and flowers, painted with thick lines, marked a new creation in artistic interpretation. The emperor gave particular attention to depicting realistic expressions. His *Bird and Loquat Tree* was a masterpiece which demonstrated his realistic emphasis based on thick lines and augmented with meticulously executed details and a natural blend of careful painting style and delicate sketching. Every part of the painting spoke of vitality. By using a different degree of wetness in the colors, and combining both light and dark hues, the emperor created an immensely impressive mood. He used light watercolors to create the images of the loquat

50

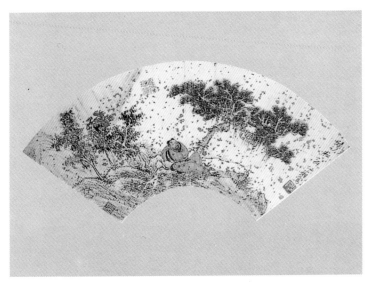

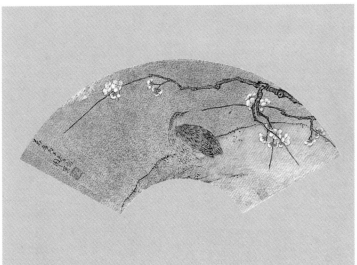

Top: Sleeping Under a Pine Tree After Drinking (Song Yin Zui Wo) by Yao Shou of the Ming Dynasty.
Bottom: Plum Blossoms and a Quail (Mei Hua An Chun) by Zhou Zhimian of the Ming.

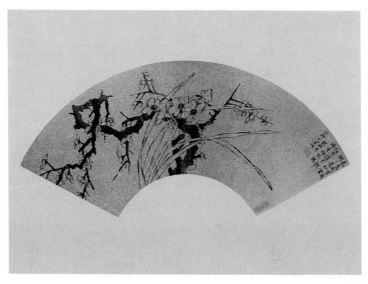

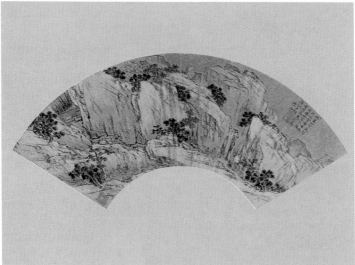

Top: Narcissus and Plum Blossoms (Shui Xian Chun Mei) by Wang Guxiang of the Ming Dynasty.
Bottom: Autumn Mountain Scene (Qiu Shan Huang Ye) by Lu Zhi of the Ming.

fruit and then thick ink to portray the flower, thus achieving the effect of vibrancy. Next he used both light and thick colors to reflect the front and back of the leaves so as to give the two loquat trees a charming gracefulness. For the bird and butterfly, he used a combination of thick and thin lines and wet and dry ink to bring out their vividness. The butterfly seems to be darting about freely among the tree branches, oblivious of the bird watching from behind. A battle of life and death seems about to break out at any given moment. This image of "action hidden in stillness" fully reflects natural life.

A silk fan bearing the picture *Sunflower and Butterfly of the Song* (Song Kui Hua Xia Die) unearthed from the tomb of Zhu Tan in Zouxian, Shandong, in 1970, has a golden background to the illustra-

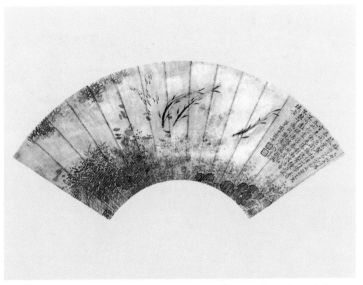

Fish Swimming Among Grass (Zao Ying Yu Xi) by Yun Shouping of the Qing Dynasty.

Top: Landscape painted by Yan Shengsun.
Bottom: Landscape painted by Hong Wu.

54

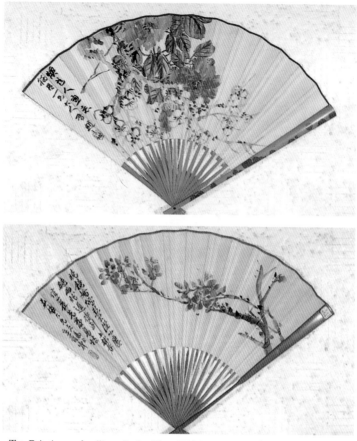

Top: Painting and calligraphy by Zhao Zhiqian of the Qing Dynasty.
Bottom: Peach Blossoms and calligraphy by Wu Changshuo of the Qing Dynasty.

Left Top: Aged Trees on Sturdy Rocks (Chong Yan Gu
Cui) by Dai Xi of the Qing Dynasty.
Left Center: Autumn Forest by Chen Mei.
Left Bottom: Landscape painted by Huang Binhong of
the Qing Dynasty.

tion of the sunflower and butterfly. The painting is accompanied by two red seals while the back of the fan contains a four-line poem written by Emperor Gaozong of the Song Dynasty. The calligraphy of the emperor shows well-composed and beautifully written characters which compliment the painting.

On October 13, 1949, workers found in the south warehouse in the Hall of Preserving Heart of the Forbidden City, a large folding fan with 15 pieces of bones in its frame and carrying a painting by Emperor Xuande of the Ming Dynasty. The bones of the fan were 33 inches long, giving the fan spread a length from top to bottom of 24 inches and a width from left to right of 60 inches. At the time it was discovered, the fan frame and spread had already become badly damaged. Careful repair by experienced artisans has restored the splendor of the original work, which contains the personal handwriting of the emperor. On each side of the fan is a painting of human figures. Both sides carry seals announcing that the fan was once owned by emperors of the Ming and Qing dynasties. One side also has written characters to the effect that it was completed in the Hall of Military Grace in the spring of the second year under Xuande's reign. These seals and words prove that the artist of the painting was Emperor Xuande of the Ming who reigned from 1426 to 1435. Completed in the second year of his reign (1427), this fan is a real treasure, being one of the earliest painted folding fans still in existence.

High officials during China's dynastic period occupied important social positions, standing below the emperor but above millions of citizens. Though many officials, such as prime ministers and senior statesmen, left a wealth of poems, calligraphic works, and articles, such works on fan spreads are seldom seen.

A fan with a poem written by Wang Ao (1450-1524) of the Ming Dynasty is one of the rare items in the Shanghai Museum. It is written in a flowing hand. Wang Ao was a native of Suzhou, who worked his way up to the position of the chief minister after first doing well in the successive imperial examinations for selecting officials. His poem is well written, and his flowing handwriting style expresses strength and determination. No wonder, Tang Bohu (also known as Tang Yin), a famous painter, praised Wang Ao as someone "whose articles were the best" and as a prime minister "not to be compared."

A folding fan with a gold paste surface, along with 13 parts of the bamboo bone frame, was unearthed from the tomb of Xu Yufu of the Ming Dynasty in Wuxian, Suzhou. On the top side of the fan two poems were written in the flowing-script style of Shen Shixing. Shen (1535-1614), a native of Suzhou, was known for his mastery of the flowing hand and this fan is thus a rare treasure. He did very well in the imperial examinations in 1561 and even better the following year when he emerged as the top scholar. From there he embarked on the road of officialdom to eventually become chief minister.

In December 1966, two fans were found in the tomb of Wang Xijue (1534-1610) and his wife in suburban Suzhou. One of the folding fans, designed for a man, was 11 inches long with 16 pieces of watermill polished bamboo bones for its frame. The paper fan spread had decayed. The other fan, a lady's fan, was also 11 inches long with 22 pieces of bamboo bones that had a black lacquer finish. The fan spread, in black background with gold dots, carried diamond-shaped patterns in gold. This spread was better preserved and had sparkling images. Wang Xijue was a native of Taicang, Jiangsu, and became the chief minister in 1584. He was also known as a superb calligraphy.

Those scholars who wished to achieve the top place in the imperial examinations had to prove themselves in two ways: writing good articles and doing beautiful calligraphy. As a result, the fans owned by the examination candidates who took the top placement honors were excellent works that combined poetry, prose, and calligraphy.

The first man to achieve the top position in the first imperial examination held during the Qing Dynasty was Fu Yijian (1609-65). A native of Liaocheng in Shandong, he emerged as the top candidate in 1646. Fu was known for his folding fan which had a gold paste spread on which he wrote prose together with a poem in seventeen lines.

During the early years of the Qing Dynasty, the bold, free-style of writing was popularly represented by such scholars as Wang Tuo, Song Cao, and Fu Yijian. But during the 17th century, as the Ming Dynasty was being replaced by the Qing, a period of spiritual vacuum was occurring. Those of strong individual character would inevitably take the opportunity to express themselves, and calligraphy was one of the best means through which to pour out their feelings and thoughts. Fu Yijian was known to be a diligent writer and someone

Top: Admiring the Moon (Shang Yue Tu) by Wang Wen of the Ming Dynasty.
Bottom: Calligraphy in cursive script by Wang Wen of the Ming Dynasty.

Left Top: Peony by Tang Yin of the Ming Dynasty.
Left Center: Landscape by Shen Zhou of the Ming Dynasty.
Left Bottom: A Solitary Man Sitting by the River by Qian Gu of the Ming Dynasty.

who did not lose all standards when freely expressing himself. The calligraphy on his fan was an exact example of his character in this respect.

Qian Qi (1742-99) from Suzhou in Jiangsu, took first place in each of the three levels of the civil service examinations, all the way from the township and provincial level to the final imperial examinations held in the Forbidden City. His excellent performance won him the praise of Emperor Qianlong (r. 1736-1795), one of the greatest of all Qing emperors. He was particularly well-known for his seventeen-line prose and poetry on the white spread of a folding fan. In calligraphic style, Qian studied the work of Ouyang Xun and Li Beihai of the Tang Dynasty, both characterized as being very disciplined but highly expressive. Though Qian appeared quite modest, his work spoke of confidence. It was this writing style that made his fan in particular a representative work.

There is a unique fan by five top scholars with a gold paste background and which carried a thirty-six line poem created by Pan Shien, Wu Qirui, Zhu Changyi, Lin Hongnian, and Niu Fubao. Until that time people had never seen any fan like this: with the calligraphic work of five top imperial examination winners on a single fan spread, each complementing yet offsetting the other. Wu Qirui had simulated the calligraphic style of the legendary Mi Fu and the more recent Liang Shanzhou, which was highly beautiful and expressive. Zhu Changyi's writing was quite disciplined but by no means dull. Lin Hongnian strictly followed the style of Ouyang Xun, and his writing was meticulous in every detail. Niu Fubao pursued a style of solemnity. Pan might be said to be the best of, as his style combined both free expression and discipline, being bold and gentle, solemn and modest, and individually graceful yet illuminating.

What made this fan particularly unique was the fact that the five scholars had taken the imperial examinations in different years, stretching over a period of 45 years from the first to the last.

A white background fan of Liu Chunlin (1872-1944), the last top winner of the imperial examinations in the Qing Dynasty, contained an article and a poem totaling twenty-nine lines. Liu was a native of Hebei and he won the top place in 1904, the last person to do so because only seven years later the dynastic rule was overthrown in the Revolution of 1911, which saw the founding of the Republic of China and the abolishment of the examination system. Liu inherited the calligraphic style of the Tang Dynasty and his writings were steady and disciplined, but not stiff. He used the brush with a careful sensitivity and the ink—used for different lines and characters—appeared quite balanced. Liu's writings demonstrated a smooth and harmonious beauty as well as peaceful and tranquil expression.

In *The Collected Calligraphic Works of Seventy Qing Dynasty Top Imperial Examination Winners*, compiled by Wu Hufan, Liu Chunlin's writing is featured in the opening chapter. Wu spent more than twenty years obtaining the fans of top imperial scholars, either by spending huge sums to buy them outright, or by exchanging the antiques he owned or his own paintings and calligraphy in trade. He later had their authenticity appraised and acknowledged, wrote annotations for each fan, and mounted them in a one-volume collection. This work he presented to the city of Suzhou, his home town, in 1959, to mark the tenth anniversary of the founding of the People's Republic of China. When he gave this work to Qian Yong of the Cultural Relics Administration of Suzhou, who happened to be a relative of his, Wu asked Qian Yong to continue to collect the fans that were owned by the leading imperial examination winners. For decades since then, Qian Yong has searched for more fans in this category. He has studied thousands upon thousands of paintings and at least a thousand fans, but has so far been unable to discover a single work that can match the quality of the fans in Wu's collection.

During the Ming Dynasty, four scholars named Tang, Shen, Wen, and Qiu, who began their careers as artists of painting and calligraphy, gradually began to put their work on fans. People in Suzhou at that time showed the greatest interest in painted fans, which they no longer kept for practical use but rather kept in collections for admiration. Gradually, this became a local custom and way of life. This spurred the wave of fan collecting and the practice of buying plain, unadorned fans and then asking artists to paint or write on them. The Drifting Cloud Tower in Suzhou was unique in terms of the number of fans in its collection that had been painted or written on by famous artists. At that time, it had sixteen golden background fan spreads by these four famous artists. Bound into collections, each of the works by these

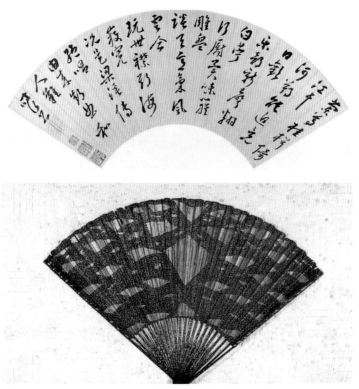

Top: Calligraphy by Shen Shixing in cursive script.
Bottom: Gold pattern on black ink background by Wang Xijue.

63

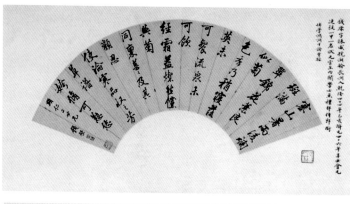

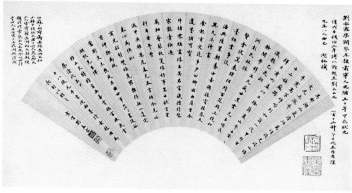

artists was a masterpiece. There was also a ten-piece collection of golden background fan spreads known as *Nine Friends in Paintings*. In addition, the Tower had works by the "Six Top Artists" of the early Qing Dynasty, by the "Four Wangs" (Wang Shimi, Wang Jian, Wang Hui and Wang Yuanqi), as well as a collection of fan spreads by Wu Li and Yun Shouping.

A golden background fan spread, entitled *Landscape*, painted by Shen Zhou (1427-1509), a native of Suzhou and one of the founders of the Wumen school of painting during the Ming Dynasty, depicts a river of limpid water against distant hills and houses with thatched roofs beyond an arched bridge visible in the foreground. This was often a typical scene in the area around Suzhou. Through his steady use of the brush, Shen Zhou created a peaceful and serene atmosphere.

The golden background fan spread, entitled *Peony*, was created by Tang Yin (1470-1523). A native of Suzhou, Tang was also known as Tang Bohu. He began as a landscape artist, but painting flowers and birds was fashionable in his day. In his works on peonies, flowers, and leaves, the objects, though quite dense, were well laid out. Tang used thick brushes and rendered bright colors, achieving an effect of beauty and strength. He was famous for his unique style among the Wumen school of artists.

Another golden background spread has a poem by Wen Zhengming (1470-1559). Wen was a native of Suzhou and was also known as the "Recluse of Hengshan". After the death of Shen Zhou, Wen became the leader of the Wumen school. This seven-character-per-line poem was written in a handwriting style that was between the flowing and cursive style, and demonstrates plain yet strong characteristics. Wang Chong of the Ming Dynasty also produced a five-character-per-line poem on a fan with a golden background.

Admiring the Moon (Shang Yue Tu), a painting on a golden background by Wang Wen, is vividly portrayed with clearly defined levels of ink and a composition of carefully designed objects and perfect placement. This was another example of fan spread art created by writing a poem in flowing hand on a golden background, which won acclaim due to its steady and forceful features.

Qian Gu (1508-?), a student of Wen Zhengming, painted *A Soli-*

tary Man Sitting by the River on the golden background of a fan spread. The clever combination of dots and lines in an uninhibited painting style resulted in a scene giving a viewer much room for imagination.

Orchid, painted by Zhou Tianqiu on the golden background of a fan spread, is a work of flowing beauty. The artist created a piece of balanced density and clearly composed structure. His calligraphy of a poem on another golden background fan spread had a compact structure and was done in elegant handwriting.

Fishing at Xishan, painted by Sun Zhi on a cold gold background, created a lovely image with the use of dots and a very economical range of changes.

Dong Qichang (1555-1636) from Shanghai was the leader of the Huating school of art that has influenced the Chinese field of calligraphy for hundreds of years. Among other works, he was known for his flowing hand calligraphy of a poem with seven characters in each line that he inscribed on the golden background of a fan spread.

Ni Yunlu worked on both sides of a fan spread. On one side he painted the scene of a hill and pine trees in peace and tranquility with light colors, while on the other side he wrote a poem about strength and determination. Ni regarded this as a representative work of his for both sides of the fan suggested the characteristics of a famed gentleman and scholar.

Landscape in Imitation of Huang Zijiu by Xiang Shengmo, painted on the golden background of a fan spread, is a rare work by the artist. In it he used thick lines to bring forward a small river that meanders its way among pine trees. Behind the trees is a mountain villa.

Catching a Butterfly was painted by Chen Hongshou on the golden background of a fan spread. Depicting a fan within a fan, the composition is unique and rightly combines the idea of a real fan and an image of a fan. On the left is a butterfly while on the right is a lady. The image of the lady is rather exaggerated and her costume is highly decorative. The artist used a "three whites" method to paint her face so as to create the impression that she had worries she could not escape from. She is vividly portrayed in her attempt to catch a darting butterfly that appears true to life. The realistic and vivid images have made this painting a masterpiece.

Trees and Rocks by Wang Shouqi, on the golden background of a

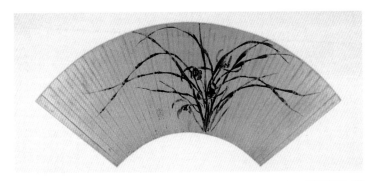

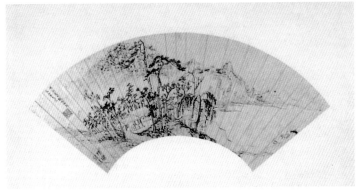

Top: *Orchid* painted by Zhou Tianqiu.
Bottom: *Landscape* by Hou Maogong.

Right Top: Calligraphy by Wen Zhengming.
Right Center: Rocks and Trees painted by Wan Shouqi.
Right Bottom: Fishing at Xishan by Sun Zhi.

67

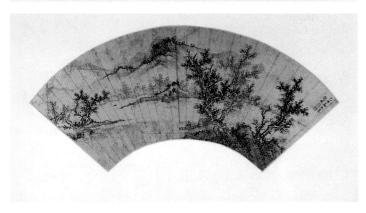

fan spread, portrays grotesque rocks and sturdy trees. The poetic thickness of the ink gives the scene vitality, while the entire painting is relatively compact.

Cornel Bay of Guangling is a masterpiece combining poetry, calligraphy, and painting on a white fan spread by Yuan Ji (1642-1705) of the Qing Dynasty. Also known by the name Shitao, this native of Guangxi was originally named Zhu Ruoji. He later became a monk and took the religious name Yuan Ji. When he painted this fan he was seventy years old. This work accentuates the theme of tranquility.

Another fan bearing a painting with the title *Landscape in Imitation of Huang Zijiu*, done by Wang Yuanqi, was created when the artist was sixty-eight years old, at a time when he was most mature in his art. Wang could paint graceful, undulating scenery and was so skilful with the movement of the brush that people referred to his brush as a "golden tipped pen."

Li Xian and five others together painted *Flowers and Fruits* on the white background of a fan spread, which was a rather unusual piece of collective work. The painting bears evidence of a gathering of famous artists and calligraphers in the year 1729 in Yangzhou, Jiangsu. Each of the six artists painted just one part, but all of them demonstrated their profound attainments and skill. Apart from its artistic value, the painting is also of significance as a valuable historical document.

Xie An on a Tour by Huang Shen was painted on a golden background when the artist was forty years old. Employing a very meticulous style, the artist completed this work without the slightest hint of carelessness. He took care of every detail of the figures and their clothes with minutely executed lines, giving the work a vivid and true-to-life finish.

Bamboo and Rock in the Style of Ni Zan was painted by Gao Xiang on the white background of a fan spread. Though the artist stated that he did the painting in imitation of the work of Ni Zan, he poured all his creative skills into the painting and copied every detail of the original, a fact that demonstrated a serious and honest approach.

Aged Trees on Sturdy Rocks was painted by Dai Xi on a golden background of a fan spread. He rendered thatched houses under trees on a flat terrace that was part of a mountain cliff. In the distance are rolling mountain ranges grown with thick trees. The structure of the painting indicates a theme popular in the Song Dynasty, but the artist's use of thick ink shows a skill typical of the Yuan Dynasty.

Landscape, completed by Huang Binhong (1864-1955) on a golden background of a folding fan spread, was a window to his resourcefulness during the middle ages. He was also known for his rich experience and steadiness when he reached ninety years of age. This painting was actually completed when he was somewhat younger, and it is a work of uninhibited, elegant expression and plain style.

The above examples are but only fragments from the rich pool of painting on fans. Their splendor and superb workmanship will be cherished by countless generations. From their first appearance to the present, fans and the art of fan painting have benefited from the cre-

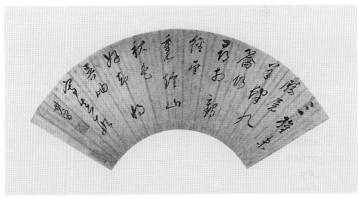

Calligraphy by Dong Qichang in cursive script.

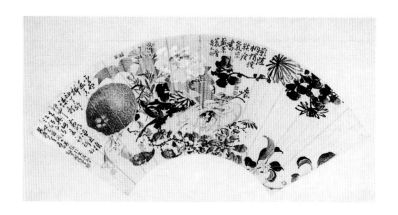

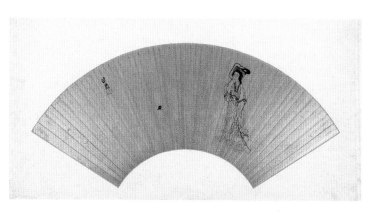

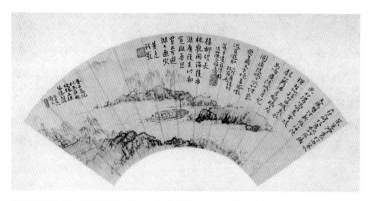

Top: Cornel Bay of Guangling (Guang Ling Zhu Yu Wan Tu) by Yuan Lo.
Bottom: Xie An on a Tour (Xie An You You Tu) by Huang Shen.

Left Top: Fan painting by Li Xian, Chen Zhuan, and four others.
Left Center: Landscape in Imitation of the Work of Huang Zijiu by Xiang Shengmo.
Left Bottom: Catching a Butterfly (Pu Die Tu) by Chen Hongshou.

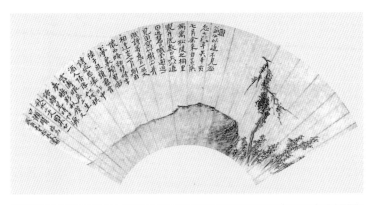

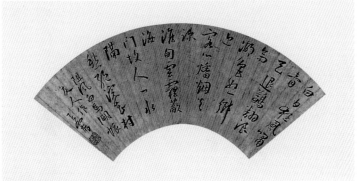

Top: Landscape in Imitation of the Work of Ni Zan by Gao Xiang.
Bottom: Calligraphy by Wang Chong.

Right Top: Calligraphy by Pan Shien and other four top
imperial examination winners.
Right Center: Calligraphy in cursive script by Chen Chun.
Right Bottom: Calligraphy in cursive script by Wu Weiye.

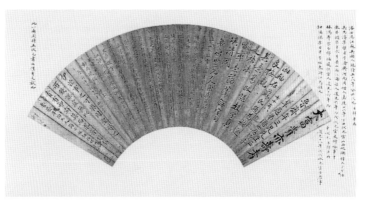

ativity of many schools. Blending the essence of the styles of various times, the art of fan making has been able to flourish and develop over time to the delight of all people.

9. The Collection and Protection of Fans

*A*ny collector will have their own favorite subjects and purpose for collecting. This is true, as well, for those collecting fans. Some of the major considerations in collecting fans are that they must be genuine, superb in quality, and in almost-new condition with no restoration work required.

Collectors endeavor to ensure that the fans they acquire are genuine by thorough knowledge of the times in which they are said to have been made, as well as knowledge of the artists who made them. Thus the collectors are able to decide whether a fan is original or a later imitation. The collectors also have to determine the era in which a fan frame and spread were made. In doing so, they analyze two aspects: the artwork on the fan and the process by which it was made. Take painted fans, for example. A newly made spread can be attached to an old frame, or vice versa. To judge the date when a frame was made, one has to examine its materials and decide whether it is bamboo, wood, ivory, horn, lacquer, or something else. The features of the manufacturing processes used in various eras must be determined. One has to look at such factors as methods of carving, the application of the lacquer, and the rendering of the paintings and calligraphic works, comparing these to other examples to decide whether the fans are originals or imitations. Finally, one has to establish the time period in which a particular fan was created.

The appraisal of fan spreads is more complicated as they are put into two categories: those valued for their manufacturing and those valued for painting and calligraphy. Fans with painting and calligraphy are the most popular among collectors. Such fans need to be appraised in the same fashion as are regular paintings and calligraphy. In other words, one needs to be armed with the knowledge of how to judge traditional painting and calligraphy. Zhang Xian, an expert at appraising painting and calligraphy, once said: "The basic conditions for appraising calligraphy and painting are knowledge of the styles of the times in which they were created and the individual styles of artists. In addition, one needs to study the seals of the artist, the paper, the silk, the introductions written on the work, the collector's seals, the methods of mounting, and also the books of the era."

These are factors for appraising painted fans as well. Those fan lovers who have just become collectors naturally have to rely on the sharp eyes of cultural appraisers. It is this area that collectors—whether novice or experienced—must be absolutely clear about the source of any so-called cultural relic or heirloom.

The best fans should be outstanding masterpieces by artisans and artists, but genuine fans may not always be the best, for each artist or artisan had his period of development. Even when they were most mature in their skills, artists still often did some quick works in order to satisfy the demand for fans by their superiors or friends. Furthermore, some well-established artists or artisans in their pursuit of money often did quite rough jobs, turning out works of inferior quality. As a result, really good works are difficult to find. For any famous artist, the top quality works are always in a minority. Quality is thus the real test of the eye of the collector and a measurement for the standards of art. Conversely, good quality does not necessarily mean that the works are genuine. Throughout the dynasties there were artists of high standards, but in the absence of people who recognized their skills, they had to make their living by copying the work of others. The highest quality works are therefore bound to be elegant and to the liking of all people.

Even when real or of top quality, collectors ' items have to be in almost-new condition in order to draw attention. Of course being new is only a relative matter. Sometimes fans of several hundred or nearly a thousand years of age may have been well-preserved. Any damage to them will cause them to lose their beauty. If such fans can be restored, they will still be valuable.

To be in almost-new condition means that the fan has to have a good appearance and be in solid form. Painted fans, in particular, need to have very fine paintings. In other words, the painting or calligraphy has to completely reflect an artists' style and attainments. The poorest examples will have blurred or abstract features that make it impossible to show the style of the artist and the features of the work. Still worse are those fans in which the spread has become torn, stained, or otherwise ruined. Some fan spreads, though in poor condition, carry paintings or calligraphy by famous artists. In such circumstances, the factor that needs to be considered is the cost required to repair and restore them. Thus, being in an almost-new condition is basic to judging a collectors' item. In the collection of any fan or its spread, being in almost-new condition and having a good physical form is a prerequisite.

The character of a fan being genuine, excellent in quality, and in almost-new condition not only reflects its artistic, historic, and scientific value, but also determines its economic value.

The protection of fans involves protecting them when they become collectors' items as well as when they are being used.

Collectors accumulate valuable examples of complete fans, fan frames, and fan spreads. Complete fans include both round fans with handles and folding fans. In the case of the fans with handles, these are usually stored in boxes of about the size of the fans in order to keep them in safe condition. The boxes may be square, rectangular, or hexagonal with a solid support inside them. Folding fans are normally kept in sheathes. In the case of the fan frames, collectors usually put ten of them in a single box. These boxes are rectangular and contain a solid device to keep the frames steady. Fan spreads are often bound together as pages of a book, or kept as single sheets. For those that are bound, the binding will be along the top rather than along the side. Round fan spreads will be mounted and then bound. Collectors can then open the pages from the left side and turn each one to the right. In most cases, the fan spreads will be set onto the surface of the pages on which they are mounted so as to protect their surfaces.

The materials used to make fans range from paper and silk to bamboo, wood, ivory, and animal horn. Their sheathes, or boxes, can also be made of paper, silk, or cotton cloth. Special attention needs to be paid to temperature and moisture. A low temperature, dry environment with strong sunlight will easily cause to the fans to break or bend. A high level of moisture allows bacteria to grow easily. Besides, damage by insects and rats can be highly destructive. Needless to say, precious fans have to be kept in places away from the sunshine and with adequate ventilation. Poisons for insects should also be placed near to the fans, or the fans can be placed in camphor-wood chests. Plastic bags should never be used. Experienced collectors will wrap their fans in old newspapers before they put them in boxes, because newspapers admit air and the ink on the paper is a preventative against insects. However, when fans are wrapped in newspapers for a relatively long period of time, it is considered wise to change the paper occasionally. The use of newspapers for this purpose is most economical, and yet a highly effective and easy way to protect the fans.

At certain times of the year precious fans should be checked – in the fall in Suzhou and Hangzhou, for instance. Checking them not only gives the collector an opportunity to view the fans, but also allows them to opened and briefly exposed to the fresh air.

Under certain circumstances fan collectors will display their collection for others to see. Those who wish to do so must wear gloves. One should never examine precious fans when they are eating, let alone when they are smoking. If one holds such a precious fan, one should not lean too close to it so as to avoid any harm that might come from breathing on it. Furthermore, no drinks should be displayed on the viewing stand so as to avoid possible spillage.

When one holds a collectors ' fan, one should make sure they do not treat it as they might an ordinary fan, flapping it open or throwing it around, as this may result in damage.

The protection of fans needs to be adapted to specific conditions and done with extreme care. It is never easy to be a fan collector because this requires financial means, standards of appreciation, skills for safekeeping, and the ability to locate good fans.

Chronological Table of Chinese Dynasties

Five August Emperors	c.30th-21st century B.C.
Xia Dynasty	c.21st-16th century B.C.
Shang Dynasty	c.16th-11th century B.C.
Zhou Dynasty	c.11th century-221 B.C.
Western Zhou Dynasty	c.11th century-771 B.C.
Eastern Zhou Dynasty	770-256 B.C.
Spring and Autumn Period	770-476 B.C.
Warring States Period	475-221 B.C.
Qin Dynasty	221-207 B.C.
Han Dynasty	206 B.C.-A.D. 220
Western Han Dynasty	206 B.C.-A.D. 23
Eastern Han Dynasty	A.D. 25-220
Three Kingdoms Period	220-280
Jin Dynasty	265-420
Western Jin Dynasty	265-316
Eastern Jin Dynasty	317-420
Southern and Northern Dynasties	420-589
Sui Dynasty	581-618
Tang Dynasty	618-907
Five Dynasties	907-960
Song Dynasty	960-1279
Northern Song Dynasty	960-1127
Southern Song Dynasty	1127-1279
Liao Dynasty	916-1125
Kin Dynasty	1115-1234
Yuan Dynasty	1271-1368
Ming Dynasty	1368-1644
Qing Dynasty	1644-1911